detox

home spa
detox

Josephine Collins

RYLAND
PETERS
& SMALL
LONDON NEW YORK

Designer Sarah Fraser
Senior Editor Clare Double
Picture Researcher Tracy Ogino
Production Susannah Straughan
Art Director Gabriella Le Grazie
Publishing Director Alison Starling

First published in the United Kingdom in 2005
by Ryland Peters & Small
20–21 Jockey's Fields
London WC1R 4BW
www.rylandpeters.com

Text, design and photographs
© Ryland Peters & Small 2005
10 9 8 7 6 5 4 3 2 1

Printed and bound in China

ISBN 1 84172 850 0

A CIP record for this book is available from
the British Library.

If you are in any doubt about your health,
please consult your doctor before making
any changes to your usual dietary and
wellbeing regime. Essential oils are very
powerful and potentially toxic if used too
liberally. Please follow the guidelines and
never use the oils neat on bare skin,
unless advised otherwise. This book is
not suitable for anyone during pregnancy.

contents

introduction

Our bodies have to deal daily with a huge array of pollutants. We don't always get enough exercise or sleep. Processed foods, too much fat and sugar, caffeine and alcohol – all take their toll on our health. If environmental and dietary toxins build up in the body, they contribute to fatigue, weight gain, allergies, headaches, skin eruptions, digestive disorders, slow mental processes and a weakened immune system.

The body has its own purifying system, but if this becomes overworked and overloaded, a body detox may be the answer. It needn't be hard – you can make it a short blast over a weekend or do it gradually over a couple of weeks. There are natural power tools such as herbs and essential oils to make detoxing easier, and treatments to rejuvenate tired skin and lifeless hair. By combining a detox diet, regular exercise and better-quality sleep with these helpers, you will not only expel toxins from your body but also increase your energy, lift your mood and feel more attractive.

A journey of a
thousand miles
must begin with
a single step.
Lao-Tzu

prepare

diet

A balanced diet is the only way to make sure your body gets what it requires for optimum health. This means consuming food and drink that fulfils nutritional needs and allows your body to maintain its normal functions.

STRATEGY FOR HEALTHY EATING

- Eat regularly.

- Choose **FRESH, WHOLE FOODS** – the nearer foods are to their natural state, the more nutritious they are.

- Choose **LOW-FAT** varieties of dairy products, lean meat and any type of fish.

- Keep fats and oils to a minimum, aiming mainly for **UNSATURATED FATS**.

- Eat plenty of fresh **FRUIT AND VEGETABLES**.

- Keep treats such as chocolate, cakes, biscuits and crisps to a minimum.

- Drink plenty of **WATER**.

- Limit your intake of caffeine and alcohol.

- Vary your diet.

the power of H$_2$O

Water is needed for every chemical reaction in the body; without enough water our bodies cannot function efficiently. If we are even slightly dehydrated, it can affect how good we feel mentally, emotionally and physically, and how well we are able to work. Water helps to absorb and transport nutrients and to flush out waste from our bodies. When detoxing, the level of toxins we release is higher than normal, so we need to drink even more water than ever.

Although tap water is perfectly safe to drink, throughout any detox diet try to use filtered water for both drinking and cooking. If you prefer to drink bottled water, choose a still water with a low mineral and sodium content. Some sources of spring water are treated to meet hygiene standards, so may not necessarily be better than filtered water.

drink more water

For optimal health, drink eight glasses of filtered water a day, equivalent to about 2 litres (4 pints). When detoxing, aim to increase your water intake by following these tips.

- Drink a glass of water **FIRST THING** in the morning when you wake up and last thing in the **EVENING** before going to bed.

- Get into the habit of keeping a bottle of water within **EASY REACH** during the day.

- Increase your intake of **FRESH FRUIT** and vegetables; both have a high water content as well as many other health benefits.

enjoy your sleep

Adequate sleep is vital to wellbeing. It gives your body an opportunity for rest and renewal, and is particularly important at times when your physical systems are working hard to clear out toxins.

TIPS FOR BETTER SLEEP

- **RELAX IN A WARM BATH** Take time to relax your muscles and calm your mind by enjoying a soothing bath.

- **RELEASE YOUR WORRIES** Write down your worries and concerns before going to sleep. Give yourself permission to let go and sleep with a clear mind.

- **HAVE A SOOTHING DRINK** Sipping a milky drink or a sleep-enhancing herbal tea will help to calm your body and mind and put you in the mood for sleep.

- **LISTEN TO RELAXING MUSIC** Listen to classical music or any that you find soothing and relaxing. Don't listen to music that arouses your emotions.

- **UNWIND WITH A GUIDED JOURNEY** Any meditation or hypnosis tape that relaxes you or enhances sleep should help you to wind down and clear your mind.

refresh your skin

Exfoliating helps to remove dead cells from your skin and cleans your pores. Its stimulating action improves blood and lymph circulation as well as the appearance of the skin. Any kind of exfoliant will do. You could choose a loofah, a glove or a brush, ideally one made from natural fibres. Exfoliate in the morning in the shower, before adding salt to the bath or before a massage.

Beginning with your feet, gently work the loofah, glove or brush up your legs in long sweeping strokes. Then, starting with your hands, move up your arms before attending to the lower part of your torso, moving upwards towards your heart. This should take no more than 5 minutes, and you should do it once or twice a week. If it is making your skin sore, or your skin stings when you apply oil or cream afterwards, you may be exfoliating too vigorously or too often, so stop for a while.

soak yourself in sea salt

Taking a bath with sea salt encourages elimination of toxins through the skin. Add the following salt and oils to a warm bath and soak in it for at least 20 minutes.

1 handful of sea salt
3 drops of lemon essential oil
3 drops of grapefruit essential oil
3 drops of lavender essential oil

cleanse your face

Use a simple face mask to unblock your pores and improve your complexion. Gently heat 4 tablespoons plain oatmeal in 100 ml water until it becomes a paste. Let it cool, then mix in 2 tablespoons honey. Smooth the mask thickly onto your face, avoiding the eye area. Leave for 20 minutes, then rinse off with plenty of warm water and pat your face dry.

rejuvenate your hair

To detox your hair and leave it shiny and
feeling fresh, follow this routine. First
shampoo and rinse your hair thoroughly.
Put four chamomile teabags in a bowl,
along with 1 tablespoon fresh rosemary.
Pour over half a litre (1 pint) of boiling
water. Leave to cool for 15 minutes, then
add 1 tablespoon cider vinegar. Remove
the teabags and the rosemary by pouring
the liquid through a strainer, then pour
the strained liquid over your hair. Massage
it into your scalp and rinse out thoroughly
with plenty of warm water.

massage

Massage improves circulation and helps your body to release toxins. Self-massage can be useful if you suffer from fatigue, insomnia, muscle tension, circulatory disorders or skin problems. You can massage yourself slowly and gently, to encourage relaxation and improve circulation, or quickly, with more pressure, to counteract fatigue. Be very careful when massaging any areas that look red or are sore.

self-massage techniques

Begin a self-massage by gently stroking the skin, using two hands, alternating the strokes. You can use any of the following techniques.

- **RUBBING** To stimulate circulation and release muscle tension, rub your muscles in a circular motion with your palms or fingers.

- **KNEADING** Knead your muscles as if you are kneading bread dough.

- **TAPPING** Use rhythmic knocking or light slapping with the flat of your hand to improve blood circulation and to help relax your muscles.

- **STROKING** When you have completed your massage, end by stroking your skin gently, moving the strokes slowly outwards.

meditation

Meditation creates a focused but relaxed mind. Its benefits include improved concentration, increased self-awareness and an enhanced ability to cope with stress. All you need is a simple method that suits you. As a start, try this easy candle meditation after taking a soothing bath or shortly before going to bed. Allow 10–20 minutes.

CANDLE MEDITATION

Sit on the floor or on a chair in a darkened room with a **CANDLE LIT IN FRONT OF YOU** at eye level. Breathe in slowly and gently, keeping your eyes on the flame. Try to keep your breathing calm and relaxed. As you stare at the flame, thoughts will enter your mind. When you become aware of a thought, simply let it go and return your attention to the candle flame.

After you have repeated this exercise several times, you should find your mind becoming calm and relaxed. What you are doing is **GIVING YOUR MIND A BREAK** and learning how to focus it at will. When you have finished the meditation, take a deep breath and blow out the candle. Try not to revert at once to thinking about your troubles. Let yourself feel the benefits of a clear, relaxed mind and then reflect on something positive or go to sleep.

get motivated

1   Set aside time to prepare for your detox, for example by shopping for food, and time to carry it out. This shows that you have made a commitment to yourself – and forward planning means you won't be too busy to do it.

2   Talk to yourself positively, in the form of positive affirmations such as 'I am healthy and energetic', to keep you on track with your detox.

3 Plan an indulgent treat for when you have finished. Remember that feeling good about yourself is as crucial to your physical wellbeing as doing things that are good for your body.

4 To get the full benefits of a detox, you need to find a way to deal with stress. Exercise (see pages 40–45) is a wonderful way to let go of physical stress, but sometimes you need to be able to let go and relax instead of being active. When this is the case, meditation could help (see page 22).

5 Do it now. Over the next 24 hours think about what you could do to start detoxing your body. You could reduce the amount of caffeine or chocolate you consume, for example. Choose one or more of the detox tools in this book and incorporate it into your life today.

the detox

You cannot push
anyone up a ladder
unless he be willing
to climb himself.
Andrew Carnegie

detox superfoods

During a two-week detox, you should aim to increase your intake of water, fruits, vegetables and herbs, whole grains, pulses and beans, nuts and seeds, and some oils. Many fruits and vegetables are particularly good at helping the body with the detoxing processes; they are high in water and packed full of essential vitamins and minerals. Aim to eat fruit and vegetables as fresh as possible and try to consume a high percentage of them raw, since raw food is not only higher in nutrients but it also helps to clean the gut more efficiently than cooked food. Wherever possible, choose organic produce, which should be less taxing for your body to process. On the next two pages are superfoods to include in your detox diet.

superfood	comments	beneficial effects
water	*1.5–2 litres (3–4 pints) is the recommended daily intake; increase this during a detox diet, after exercise or in hot weather*	*flushes out water-soluble toxins from your body*
vegetables	*useful detox vegetables include artichoke, asparagus, beetroot, broccoli, cabbage, carrot, celery, garlic, onion, tomato, watercress*	*support the liver and kidneys, help to cleanse the blood and improve bowel function; aim to have four portions daily when detoxing*
fruits	*useful detox fruits include apple, apricot (fresh and dried), cranberry, grapes (red and white), lemon, orange, papaya, raspberries*	*support the liver and kidneys, help to cleanse the blood and improve bowel function; aim to have four portions daily when detoxing*
herbs	*useful detox herbs include basil, chives, coriander, garlic, marjoram, oregano, parsley, rosemary, sage, thyme*	*many fresh herbs have specific detoxing effects; they can be used in cooking, added to salads or steeped in hot water to make herbal teas*

superfood	comments	beneficial effects
whole grains	*useful detox whole grains include brown rice, oats, millet, barley, quinoa; also try rice cakes, oatcakes, rye bread*	*provide fibre, vitamins, minerals, complex carbohydrates (these maintain blood sugar, preventing cravings and drops in energy levels)*
pulses and beans	*useful detox pulses and beans include lentils, chickpeas and kidney, lima, black-eye, haricot, borlotti and flageolet beans*	*great fillers that are a good source of protein, complex carbohydrates, fibre, vitamins and minerals*
seeds and nuts	*useful detox seeds and nuts include linseeds, pumpkin seeds, sunflower seeds, sesame seeds, walnuts, brazil nuts*	*good sources of protein, minerals and essential fatty acids; aim to eat 1 tablespoon of nuts or seeds, or a mixture, daily*
oils	*useful oils include cold-pressed oils made from seeds or nuts such as flaxseed (linseed), walnut, sesame and sunflower; virgin olive oil*	*aim to have 2 tablespoons of cold oil daily (unsaturated fats have a delicate chemical structure and, once heated, unhealthy substances form)*

detox dishes

Try one of these tasty recipes to kick-start your detox, and invent your own healthy dishes using the superfoods on pages 30–31.

carrot and ginger soup

2 large carrots, peeled and sliced
1 teaspoon finely chopped fresh ginger
1 large mug of water
sea salt
freshly ground black pepper

Put the carrots and ginger in a saucepan. Cover with water and bring to the boil. Simmer until the carrots are tender. Leave to cool, then liquidize. Season with salt and pepper and serve.

avocado salad

1 avocado, sliced
2 large handfuls of mixed spinach,
watercress and rocket
½ small onion
2 tomatoes
1 level tablespoon sunflower seeds
1 level tablespoon pumpkin seeds

for the dressing:
1 tablespoon extra virgin olive oil
1 teaspoon cider vinegar
1 small clove garlic, finely chopped
sea salt
freshly ground black pepper

Put the dressing ingredients in
a large salad bowl and mix. Add
the avocado, spinach, watercress,
rocket, onion and tomatoes. Toss
the salad in the dressing and
sprinkle with the seeds.

baked apple pudding

1 medium cooking apple, cored
1 level tablespoon chopped almonds
1 level tablespoon chopped dates
2 tablespoons water

Put the apple in a small
baking dish. Sprinkle the
almonds and dates in the
middle and add the water.
Bake in a preheated oven at
175°C (350°F) gas 4 until soft.

additions to a detox diet

If you're thinking about making long-term changes after your detox, a good-quality supplement can support you.

- Multivitamin supplements help to maintain your levels of **ESSENTIAL NUTRIENTS**.

- **KELP** helps to balance your metabolic rate; it is particularly useful when you are changing your diet.

- **MILK THISTLE** boosts liver function.

- **CRANBERRY** boosts kidney function.

- **LINSEEDS** help to eliminate toxins; soak 1 tablespoon in water overnight and take before breakfast.

- A **PROBIOTIC** such as acidophilus will help to create a healthy gut environment.

FOODS TO AVOID

When you detox, **CUT DOWN OR CUT OUT** your intake of any or all of the following:

- Dairy products and margarines. You can substitute organic goat's or sheep's milk products (in moderation), almond or rice milks, or organic, unsweetened soya products.

- Refined carbohydrates (white rice, white pasta, white bread).

- Pre-packaged, processed food (tins, packets and ready-meals).

- Sugar (brown and white), sweets and chocolate.

- Fizzy drinks and squashes.

- Tea and coffee.

- Alcohol.

- Pastries and biscuits.

- Deep-fried foods.

- Red meat.

two-week detox

Two weeks is a good length of time if your usual diet is rich in alcohol, caffeine and processed food. Cut down or cut out the foods on page 35 and increase your intake of water, vegetables, fruit and other detox superfoods (see pages 30–31). The aim is to boost your health and encourage your body to eliminate old toxins that have accumulated over time. If possible, stick to all the following guidelines.

- Drink eight glasses of **FILTERED WATER** a day. Use filtered water for cooking, too.

- Aim to eat four portions of **FRUIT** and four of **VEGETABLES** daily, and vary your choice to get a good mix of vitamins, minerals and antioxidants.

- Eat **WHOLE GRAINS** and give your body a rest from wheat, especially if you are prone to bloating. Increasing your intake of brown rice can boost the elimination of toxins.

- Reduce your intake of citrus fruits, because they are aggressive cleansers.

- Any **HERBAL TEA** is allowed throughout the detox.

- If you are hungry between meals, try one of the snacks on page 47.

- Take **REGULAR EXERCISE** (see pages 40–45).

- Get as much **REST** as possible.

- If you have a headache, **DRINK LOTS OF WATER** and lie down for a while before using painkillers. 'Withdrawal' headaches are common during a detox if you usually drink caffeine.

- **NURTURE YOURSELF** with herbal help and aromatherapy treatments (see pages 48–61).

- Don't smoke.

weekend detox diet

This is ideal if you don't have the time or willpower to follow a regime for long. Follow the guidelines on pages 36–37. Begin gradual adjustments a few days before, for example cutting down on coffee. Afterwards, do not go back to your old habits immediately. With any luck your liver will be cleaner, but it may also be more sensitive to the usual toxins.

ON WAKING

1 glass of hot water with a squeeze of fresh lemon juice

BREAKFAST

a large bowl of fresh fruit

MID-MORNING AND MID-AFTERNOON

1 glass of water and 1 small carton of natural soya or goat's milk yoghurt with ½ teaspoon honey, or 2 oatcakes with thinly spread hummus

LUNCH

1 glass of water
grilled fresh fish (any kind) or goat's cheese
a large green salad, sprinkled with sunflower seeds and pine nuts
a bag of sprouted alfalfa/mung beans (from health-food shops)
OR carrot and ginger soup (see page 32)

SUPPER

basil and tomato soup

3 large tomatoes, washed and skinned
1 clove garlic, crushed
1 tablespoon fresh basil, chopped
a squeeze of lemon

Liquidize the tomatoes with the garlic
and put them in a saucepan. Add
the basil and lemon. Heat gently
until simmering, then serve.

a corn on the cob with extra virgin olive oil
and freshly ground black pepper

OR avocado salad (see page 33)

BEFORE BED

1 cup of chamomile tea

exercise effectively

Exercise is an essential part of a
detox programme. Not only does
it build strength, boost energy
levels and help to reduce stress,
but it is also a good way to help
release toxins, burn calories and
keep you in good shape.

The aim of aerobic exercise (see page 44) is to get your **HEART PUMPING** and to **ELIMINATE TOXINS** from your system. You can also do spot exercises, such as sit-ups and leg raises, designed to tone particular parts of your body. If you are aware of any health reason why you might not be able to exercise safely, consult your doctor before beginning a new exercise programme.

preparation for exercise

Start every exercise session with a warm-up period of 5–10 minutes. This will help you to stretch your muscles slowly and warm up your body. Then gradually increase your level of activity. For example, begin walking slowly or march on the spot, and then pick up the pace. Next, roll your shoulders forwards and backwards five times and turn your head from one side to the other five times, and do the stretches on the page opposite. After you have finished exercising, leave 5–10 minutes for cooling down. (You can use the stretches opposite here, too.) Again, this will allow you to stretch your muscles and let your heart rate slow down gradually, which will help to prevent injury and be kinder to your body.

BEFORE AND AFTER STRETCH

Keeping your **KNEES SOFT**, gently bend forwards, sideways and backwards from the waist five times. **GRASP YOUR HANDS** behind your back and lift for a few seconds to stretch your shoulders.

To **STRETCH YOUR THIGHS**, stand up and, bending one leg behind you, grasp the ankle and bring it up towards your bottom for a few seconds, then change to the other leg. Finish by **SHAKING OUT** your arms and legs.

aerobic exercise

Ideally, you should do some type of aerobic exercise – fast walking, jogging, swimming, dancing or bicycling – for 20 minutes at least three times a week, whether or not you are detoxing.

Choose an activity that you enjoy and that you can build up slowly and gradually. Walking is popular because it is easy to fit into most people's schedules and does not require special equipment. Start with manageable, attainable exercise goals. Setting your goals too high can be frustrating, and can lead quickly to injuries or 'burnout'. If you are not used to exercising at all, then start slowly, and give yourself time to increase your stamina. If you persevere, you will quickly notice results. Make sure you increase your water intake when you exercise, since your body will be losing fluid.

troubleshooting

I find it hard to fall asleep
There are many non-addictive herbal
sleeping tablets available from
pharmacies and health-food shops.
If you also follow a suitable guided
meditation tape, the combination
can be very effective.

I find it hard to follow a detox diet even for two days
Don't chastise yourself. Let it go and try again when you're ready. Even following the diet partially will bring some benefits.

I find it hard to keep on exercising
If you allocate specific time to your exercises and do them without fail however you're feeling, you'll find that they become just another habit, like cleaning your teeth.

I get so hungry between meals
One heaped teaspoon of spirulina (mineral-rich algae) in water before lunch will help to stop cravings. As a snack, try a handful of dried apricots, a couple of rice cakes with hummus, or a bowl of plain popcorn cooked in olive oil.

Health is worth
more than learning.
Thomas Jefferson

herbal help

versatile herbs

Herbal remedies can support the body's own detoxing processes. They are available in many forms, including fresh or dried herbs for tea, and herbal supplements. The strength of different herbs and individual sensitivity can vary. Some are very powerful and should be taken with care. Herbs should not be used in therapeutic doses for more than 12 weeks, unless recommended by a qualified herbalist. If you are taking any prescribed medication, consult a qualified herbalist before taking herbal remedies.

herbal tea

Taking herbs in tea form has a double benefit, since you are combining the herbs with water, which also helps to flush out the toxins. For this reason, the herbs listed overleaf can be made into teas, although there is usually the option of taking them in the form of capsules, tablets or tinctures. Some herbs can be combined, but to avoid overloading your body stick to a combination of just two or three. If in doubt, seek the advice of a qualified herbalist.

Pour a cup of boiling water onto 1 teaspoon of dried herb or 2 teaspoons of fresh herb. Leave to steep for 10 minutes, then remove the herb by straining. Most herbal teas are usually taken as one cup three times a day.

herbs for detoxing

Here is a selection of herbs that will help to detox your body, build your immune system and relieve stress. These can all be used to make tea.

herb	physical benefits
burdock root	eliminates toxins, clears the skin, balances hormones; a liver tonic
dandelion leaf	helps to relieve urinary tract infections, skin eruptions, stomach pains; purifies the blood; a liver tonic
lemon balm	relaxes, improves digestion, relieves irritable bowels, counteracts anxiety and depression; good as an everyday drink
nettle	improves function of the small intestine, bladder and lungs, relieves allergies and asthma
rosemary	helps clear thinking, improves circulation, boosts nervous system
sage	improves digestion and bladder function; a natural antiseptic (avoid in pregnancy or if you have epilepsy)
sarsaparilla	purifies the blood, improves skin conditions such as eczema and psoriasis; a liver tonic
vervain	soothes nerves, relieves headaches and depression, aids relaxation
yarrow	eliminates toxins, encourages sweating, improves digestion, fights infection, counteracts water retention (avoid in pregnancy)
yellow dock	eliminates toxins, clears the skin, improves liver, gall bladder and bowel functions

the benefits of aromatherapy

Aromatherapy is the use of essential oils to improve physical and emotional wellbeing. Made from flowers, fruits and parts of plants, each oil has unique properties. One of the most beneficial effects of using essential oils comes from the aroma each produces. This affects the part of the brain that governs the emotions, which is why each oil has what is called an 'emotional profile' of therapeutic effects. Essential oils can also benefit the body by absorption through the skin in massage or by being added to bath water.

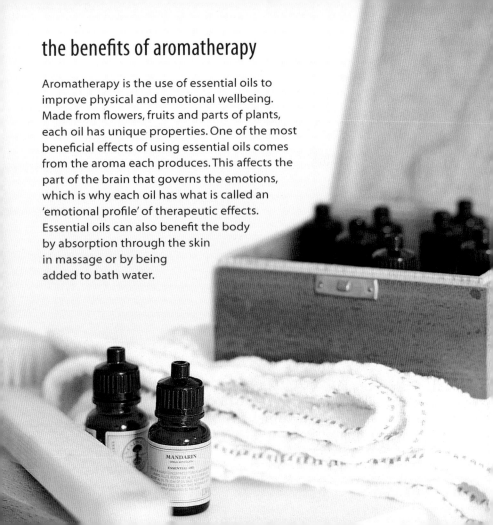

USING ESSENTIAL OILS WITH CAUTION

Since the active ingredient in an essential oil is highly concentrated, the oil should always be **DILUTED** with a base oil before being applied to the skin. Vegetable oils such as **GRAPESEED OR SOYA** are perfect for this purpose. Base oils containing vitamin E, such as jojoba and avocado, are sometimes used to make richer skin preparations, especially for dry skin.

To test your skin for **SENSITIVITY**, dab a small amount of essential oil, diluted in vegetable oil, on the inside of your wrist and leave it overnight. If there is any adverse reaction, do not use that oil.

CHILDREN under the age of 18 months should not be treated with essential oils, and they should not be taken internally or used if you are pregnant or have a medical condition such as epilepsy.

how to use essential oils

Here are some easy ways in which essential oils
can be incorporated into a detox programme.

- **BATHING** Stir 5–10 drops of essential oil into a full bath of water, after the water has finished running. It is best not to use soap with essential oils.

- **AIR FRESHENING** Add 5 drops of an essential oil to every 2 teaspoons of water in a mist spray bottle and shake before spraying.

- **MASSAGE** Make a massage oil by mixing up to 5 drops of an essential oil to every 2 teaspoons of pure vegetable oil such as grapeseed or almond.

- **STEAMING** Add 5–8 drops of essential oil to a bowl full of hot water; put a towel over your head, lean over the bowl and gently inhale the steam for about 5 minutes.

- **DIFFUSING** A diffuser is simply a small container, to which water and oil are added. A lit candle is placed underneath, and the oil's aromatic vapours fill the air as the water heats. Add 5–10 drops of essential oil to the water. If you have an electric diffuser, follow the manufacturer's instructions.

essential oils for detoxing

Many oils used in aromatherapy can be beneficial in the detoxing process.

oil	physical benefits	emotional profile
black pepper	*eliminates toxins, boosts circulation, fights infections, energizes*	*encourages moving onwards, boosts bravery, endurance*
eucalyptus	*relieves asthma, eases aching joints; a decongestant*	*boosts clear thinking, soothes heated emotions*
fennel	*eliminates toxins, relieves digestive and menopausal problems*	*helps to overcome creativity blocks, resistance to change, fear of failure*
geranium	*balances hormones, eases tension, reduces fluid retention*	*helps to relieve acute fear, heartache, lack of self-esteem, discontentment*
grapefruit	*detoxifies, energizes, relieves muscle fatigue; astringent for oily skin*	*helps to relieve self-doubt, grief, dependency, frustration*
juniper	*purifies, eliminates toxins, improves mental clarity, reduces fluid retention*	*helps to relieve guilt, discontentment, defensive behaviour*
lavender	*eases tension headaches, helps breathing, promotes sleep*	*helps to relieve insecurity, trauma, fear, addiction, obsessive behaviour*
lemon	*eliminates toxins, reduces cellulite, balances nervous system*	*helps relieve resentment, distrust, irrational thinking, apathy*
orange (sweet)	*relieves stress, reduces cellulite*	*helps to relieve apathy, worry, addiction, lethargy, depression*
sandalwood	*heals skin, reduces stress, helps breathing, promotes restful sleep*	*helps to relieve insecurity, loneliness, nightmares, dwelling on the past*
ylang ylang	*relaxes tense muscles, promotes restful sleep, lowers high blood pressure*	*helps to relieve anxiety, resentment, jealousy, frustration, anger, irritability*

10 easy ways to detox with herbs

1   Get chopping. Rosemary, sage and thyme are all good detoxing herbs to add to your cooking.

2   Try adding chopped fresh parsley instead of salt to add flavour to your food.

3   On waking, drink lemon balm tea, or try a glass of hot water with a squeeze of fresh lemon juice.

4   Drink a cup of sleep-enhancing chamomile tea before you go to bed.

5 Drink refreshing peppermint tea after meals to aid digestion.

6 Make a stress-relieving spritzer of sweet orange oil and water to freshen your home.

7 Diffuse some stimulating black pepper oil as you warm up before exercise.

8 Self-massage with ylang ylang oil to relax tired muscles.

9 Relax in a warm aromatherapy bath. Try lavender for relaxation or eucalyptus to clear your mind.

10 Treat yourself to an aromatherapy massage to make your hard work worthwhile.

useful addresses

organizations

The Herb Society
Sulgrave Manor
Sulgrave
Banbury OX17 2SD
01295 768899
www.herbsociety.co.uk

International Federation of Aromatherapists (IFA)
Stamford House
182 Chiswick High Road
London W4 1PP
020 8742 2605
www.ifaroma.org

National Institute of Medical Herbalists
56 Longbrook Street
Exeter EX4 6AH
01392 426022
www.nimh.org.uk

retailers

Boots
www.boots.com

Crabtree and Evelyn
www.crabtree-evelyn.co.uk

Heal's
196 Tottenham Court Road
London W1T 7LQ
020 7636 1666
www.heals.co.uk

John Lewis
278–306 Oxford Street
London W1A 1EX
020 7629 7711
www.johnlewis.com

Marks & Spencer
Michael House
Baker Street
London W1U 8EP
020 7935 4422
www.marksandspencer.com

Molton Brown
www.moltonbrown.co.uk

Neal's Yard Remedies
15 Neal's Yard
Covent Garden
London WC2H 9DP
020 7379 7222
www.nealsyardremedies.com

Origins
www.origins.com

Selfridges
400 Oxford Street
London W1A 1AB
0870 837 7377
www.selfridges.co.uk

SPACE.NK
37 Earlham Street
London WC2H 9LD
020 7379 7030
www.spacenk.co.uk

credits

Key: ph=photographer, a=above, b=below, r=right, l=left, c=centre

Endpapers ph David Montgomery; 1–2 ph Polly Wreford; 3 ph Henry Bourne; 4 ph Peter Cassidy; 5 ph Dan Duchars; 6a ph Andrew Wood; 6b ph Debi Treloar; 7 ph Dan Duchars; 8al ph Chris Everard / a house in Paris designed by Bruno Tanquerel (t. +33 1 43 57 03 93); 8ar ph William Lingwood; 8b–9l ph David Montgomery; 9r ph Caroline Arber; 10–11a ph Debi Treloar; 11b ph Peter Cassidy; 12 ph David Montgomery; 13l & c ph Debi Treloar; 13r–15 background ph Dan Duchars; 15 inset ph David Brittain; 16 main ph Andrew Wood; 16 inset ph Dan Duchars; 17–18a inset ph David Montgomery; 18b inset ph Debi Treloar; 18 background ph Francesca Yorke; 19l inset ph Dan Duchars; 19r inset ph David Montgomery; 19 background ph William Lingwood; 20 ph David Montgomery; 21a ph Dan Duchars; 21c ph David Montgomery; 21b–22 ph Debi Treloar; 22 inset ph David Montgomery; 23 ph David Montgomery; 24 ph James Merrell; 25 ph Polly Wreford; 26l ph William Lingwood; 26r ph Francesca Yorke; 27a ph David Brittain; 27b ph David Montgomery; 28 ph Peter Cassidy; 29a & c ph Francesca Yorke; 29bl ph Jean Cazals; 29bc ph Peter Cassidy; 29r ph Nicky Dowey; 30–31 ph Francesca Yorke; 32 inset ph Peter Cassidy; 32 main & 33 background ph William Lingwood; 33 inset ph Debi Treloar; 34 background ph Polly Wreford; 34 inset ph David Montgomery; 35 ph David Brittain; 36 background ph David Brittain; 36 inset ph Francesca Yorke; 37 background ph Polly Wreford / Mary Foley's house in Connecticut; 37a inset ph David Brittain; 37b inset ph David Montgomery; 38 ph Ian Wallace; 39 ph Debi Treloar; 40–41 ph Chris Everard; 42–43 inset ph Debi Treloar; 43 main ph David Montgomery; 44 background ph Jan Baldwin; 44a inset ph Chris Everard; 44b inset ph David Montgomery; 45 ph Chris Everard; 46 ph Debi Treloar; 47l ph Alan Williams; 47r ph Debi Treloar; 48al ph Peter Cassidy; 48ar, 48b & 49l ph Caroline Arber; 49r ph David Montgomery; 50 ph William Lingwood; 51l ph Debi Treloar; 51c ph Caroline Arber; 51r ph Dan Duchars; 52 ph William Lingwood; 53 ph Caroline Arber; 54 & 55a ph Dan Duchars; 55b ph David Montgomery; 56 ph Dan Duchars; 57–59 ph David Montgomery; 60 ph Caroline Arber; 61 ph William Lingwood; 62 ph David Montgomery; 63 ph James Merrell; 64 ph Polly Wreford.

If any thing is sacred the human body is sacred.

Walt Whitman